RANGE ROVER
CONVERSIONS

**Nick
Dimbleby**

Foulis

Haynes

Range Rover

A **FOULIS** Motoring book

First published 1987
© Nick Dimbleby 1987

Published by:
Haynes Publishing Group
Sparkford, Nr. Yeovil, Somerset
BA22 7JJ, England

Haynes Publications Inc.
861 Lawrence Drive, Newbury Park,
California 91320 USA

**British Library Cataloguing in
Publication Data**

Dimbleby, Nick
   Range Rover conversions.
   1. Range Rover Truck
   I. Title
   629.2'222   TL230.5.R3

   ISBN 0-85429-615-8

Library of Congress catalog card
number 87-82237

Editor: Robert Iles
Page layout: Peter Kay
Printed in England by: J.H. Haynes & Co.
Ltd.

Conversions

CONTENTS

Range Rover

ACKNOWLEDGEMENTS

"Thank you" to all who made this book possible; especially:

Dick Anderton	Land Rover Limited
John Perkins	A.E. Smith
H.S. Fry and Norman Trangmar	F.L.M. (Panelcraft)
Kenneth Evans and Keith Strover	Glenfrome
H.G. Lomas	Herbet Lomas Ambulances
Alan Collins	The Panther Car Co.
E.F. Collins	Wood & Pickett Limited
Chris Cackett and David Pollard	Dale Electric
Ben Moore	Wadham Stringer (Ambulances)
Mike Pick	Carmichael
Christine Musgrave	Carbodies
Karin Sullivan	Overfinch Limited
Doreen Pickering	Ogle Design
R.J. Flavel	The Automobile Association
J. Slater	Scottorn Trailers
R.J. Godfrey	Gloster Saro Limited
S.M. Greene	Pilcher Green
M.F. Cole	Malcolm Cole
H. Torosyan	Bearmach
Simon Lee	Janspeed
Keith Tolley	J.N.R. Motors
Alvin Smith	Alvin Smith
Peter Zanelli	Townley
B.J. Robinson	Symbol
Mrs. M.E. Christos	Care le Gant

- to all other other employees of other companies I had dealings with, but whose names were undisclosed.

   - to the Chief Constables of Cumbria Constabulary, Warwickshire Constabulary and the City of London Police Force, as well as, Sergeant Cook of the Avon & Somerset Police Force, Mr Goss of the Somerset Ambulance Service, Les Dyke and the Fire Department of Bournemouth International (Hurn) Airport.

   But my greatest thanks go to Simon Budd and Paul O'Connor of Land Rover Limited, without whom much of this book would not be possible.

THE RANGE ROVER

The Range Rover must be, with the exception of the Land-Rover, the world's most converted and versatile car.

Ever since its launch on the 17th June 1970, specialist converters like Scottorn, Glenfrome, Wood & Pickett, Carmichael, Pilcher Greene, Herbet Lomas and even Land-Rover itself have produced some most stunning and functional conversions for many people belonging to many walks of life.

There are many different types of conversions: Ambulances, Fire/Rescue vechicles, Military, Police and the most luxurious limousines often going into the six-figure price range.

Because the Range Rover is built so strongly, the car provides an excellent base for a stretched limousine. Also because of its four-wheel drive capabilities, it often finds itself being made into a vehicle of house-like proportions for the sandy desert plains of the Middle East, where cars are very much status symbols, and money is no object.

For everyone interested in the Range Rover marque, this book provides an insight into some of the spectacular and functional conversions that many companies are so proud to produce.

Unfortunately, the Range Rover conversion boom in the Middle East has ended, and some companies – like Carawagon – are in the hands of the receiver.

The launch into America, however, should revive the business, everyone knows how the Americans like stretched limousines . . .

Range Rover

SPECIFICATIONS

Fuel injected engine

Eight cylinders in vee formation, aluminium constructed with five-bearing crankshaft and self-adjusting tappets.

Bore	88.9 mm (3.5 in)
Stroke	71.1 mm (2.8 in)
Cubic capacity	3528 cc (215 cu in)

High compression:

Compression ratio	9.35:1
Max power (DIN net)	123 kW (165 bhp) at 4750 rpm
Max torque	280 Nm (207 lbf ft) at 3200 rpm

Low compression:

Compression ratio	8.13:1
Max power (DIN net)	112 kW (150 bhp) at 4750 rpm
Max torque	258 Nm (190 lbf ft) at 2500 rpm

Carburettor engine

Eight cylinders in vee formation, aluminium constructed with five-bearing crankshaft and self-adjusting tappets.

Bore	88.9 mm (3.5 in)
Stroke	71.1 mm (2.8 in)
Cubic capacity	3528 cc (215 cu in)

High compression:

Compression ratio	9.35:1
Max power (DIN net)	94 kW (127 bhp) at 4000 rpm
Max torque	263 Nm (194 lbf ft) at 2500 rpm

Low compression:

Compression ratio	8.13:1
Max power (DIN net)	98 kW (132 bhp) at 5000 rpm
Max torque	251 Nm (185 lbf ft) at 2500 rpm

Turbo diesel engine

Four cylinder in-line turbo-charged intercooled diesel. Cast iron crank, aluminium cylinder head with cast iron liners.

Bore	92 mm (3.622 in)
Stroke	90 mm (3.543 in)
Compression ratio	21.5:1
Max power (DIN net)	84 kW (112.6 bhp) at 4200 rpm
Max torque	248 Nm (183 lbf ft) at 2400 rpm

Conversions

Range Rover two- and four-door specifications

Length overall	4470 mm (176 in)
Height overall	1800 mm (71 in)
Width overall	1780 mm (70 in)
Wheelbase	2540 mm (100 in)
Width of axle	1490 mm (58.8 in)
Ground clearance	320 mm (12.5 in)

Weights

Two-door

	Front axle	Rear axle	Total
Unladen	893 kg	869 kg	1762 kg
EEC kerb	912 kg	983 kg	1895 kg
Gross	1000 kg	1510 kg	2510 kg

Four-door

	Front axle	Rear axle	Total
Unladen	909 kg	884 kg	1793 kg
EEC kerb	928 kg	999 kg	1927 kg
Gross	1000 kg	1510 kg	2510 kg

Towing capacity

	Trailer weight
Unbraked trailer	750 kg
Trailer with over-run brakes	3000 kg (on road)
	1000 kg (off road)
Trailer with close-coupled brakes	4000 kg (on road)
	1000 kg (off road)

Load volumes (maximum usable)

Rear seat down	1.02 m^3 (36.18 ft^3)
Rear seat up	2.00 m^3 (70.80 ft^3)

Electrical supply

Battery:
    Reserve capacity   180/78/89 A/min/V (55 Ah)
(N.B. Batteries may vary in output for specialist conversions)

Range Rover

Around the Solihull test track

My first impressions of the Range Rover Turbo D were supplied by Mr Chris Goffey, of BBC 2's *Top Gear*.

For those of you who did not see this programme, Mr. Goffey said, in short, that the Turbo D engine lacked power and needed more development.

The reason Mr. Goffey said such damning words about the Turbo D may have been that he had not been properly briefed on how to use it to the full. Rumours at Solihull say that this was probably his calendar's fault. ...

All his comments were erased from my mind while having the ride of my life around the Solihull Test Track. One minute we were being flung to the side of the vehicle while taking a hairpin bend at 50 mph, the next we were being flung towards the dashboard while coming down a one-in-one slope.

The lap record for the concrete Solihull test track is currently held by a Metro 6R4, but on certain bends and straights, I felt we were getting extremely close to beating this record. Just as I was thinking this, we stopped, and promptly drove up a rather steep earth embankment. This, I was told, is a replica of most motorway embankments. Now I can see why the Range Rover is one of the most used Police motorway units ...

We then headed for the Solihull 'Jungle'. This is a wooded area with a rather muddy track straight through the middle, with various water splashes and tilts dotted here and there.

I had never realised how leisurely off-roading is when you are a passenger, or at some places, the driver. At one stage we contemplated picking some elderberries for some elderberry wine, but we resisted the temptation and carried on.

After the 'Jungle', we then made tracks (quite muddy ones actually) to the area where all the slopes, deeper water splashes, the Solihull railway crossing and staggered bumps are situated.

On the way there we encountered a modestly sized metal 'bridge', for want of a better word. We went forwards, backwards, and forwards again over this object while I took photographs.

The first obstruction we encountered was an awesome sight, a rather steep slope made out of dirt and large stones, which I thought no vehicle could traverse. As I was thinking this, we promptly drove up with incredible ease, and came down the other side again with absolute control. We then did it again, except this time, while coming down the other side, we stopped, and promptly reversed straight up again, with only a minimal amount of effort.

Next were the staggered bumps. These the Range Rover just sailed over, with a minimum of fuss and rocking.

Following that, a deeper water splash. Although the water was way above the bottom of the doors, not a drop leaked in.

You can drive a Land or Range Rover as deep into water as you like, as long as there is an air intake above, water level.

Awkward angles followed. These were 19% to the left, and 40% to the right.

Skipping the 'Solihull Siding' (railway sleepers to drive over), the staggered bumps on a slope and some very deep ruts, the next obstacle is the one-in-one or 50% slope. This the Range Rover climbed with incredible ease (again!), and proved to me that the Range Rover must still be the best vehicle at combining comfort, speed, and outstanding four-wheel drive capability on (or off!) the road today.

Our driver was Dick Attherton of Land Rover.

Land Rover Limited,
Meteor Works,
Lode Lane,
Solihull,
West Midlands,
B92 8NW
(021) 743 4242

Range Rover

BEARMACH

Bearmach Quadruple Headlight Conversion

Resembling the American Dodge Monaco in style, the Bearmach quadruple headlight conversion is part of the enormous range of exterior options you can obtain from Bearmach.

The quadruple headlight conversion has a redesigned grille, and is available for the two- or four-door Range Rover. The vehicle pictured has an aluminium bull bar. This does not come fitted with the conversion, but is available at extra cost.

Also available from Bearmach are: gun racks, flared wheel arches, spotlights, aluminium light coverings (front and rear) and any other option to suit your need.

Bearmach UK Limited,
Bearmach House,
Maindy Road,
Cardiff,
CF2 4XN
(0222) 41313

Bearmach's quadruple headlamp conversion, pictured sporting an aluminium bull bar.

The Rugged Rider can quite happily carry two adults; so Dad can drive it too!

BIG J

Big J Rugged Rider

Not stretched, but shrunk!

This one-third replica of the Range Rover has a six horsepower engine, and can easily carry two adults. The body is constructed of glass reinforced plastic, so is quite able to withstand a few knocks from the novice driver.

The vehicle has an electric starter, front and rear lights, disc brakes, five-speed gearbox, automatic clutch, roll cage, full upholstery and a twelve-volt battery.

As well as the above standard equipment, you can order a front bull bar, seat belts and a radio/cassette player, making it even more like Mum's or Dad's!

Unfortunately you cannot buy the Rugged Rider any more, as Big J have gone out of business. Don't be too disappointed though, as Symbol of London make a similar model along with miniature Ferraris, Lamborghinis and Mercedes. The price? About the same as an Austin Metro.

Length	1735 mm (70 in)
Width	1070 mm (49 in)
Height	1040 mm (42 in)
Engine	Air cooled four-stroke engine. 221.75 cc.
Suspension	Coil spring with Panhard rods front and rear.
Wheel & Tyres:	Pressed steel eight-inch wheels. 16X6.50X8 all-terrain tyres.

The only caravan conversion for the Range Rover. The elevating roof is fully retractable.

CARAWAGON

Carawagon Series 100

Believe it or not, there is only one caravan conversion based on the Range Rover.

It is built by Carawagon, who have had a lot of experience in converting Land and Range Rovers into caravans, mobile offices and command units mainly for use by the military.

Based on the two-door, the Series 100 sleeps two people, and can accommodate six. The elevating roof provides standing room within the vehicle for cooking and washing.

Other features include: 75 cm cantilevered table, wardrobe, fluorescent light, swivelling lamps and all round curtains.

As well as the caravan conversion, Carawagon build a mobile office on a similar specification to the above.

Carbodies Unitruck, fitted with optional bull-bar. Note the roll-bar mounted spare wheel.

CARBODIES

Carbodies Unitruck

Developed as a prototype in 1982, only a few five-seat pick-ups were produced as there was not much interest in them.

The vehicle is extremely versatile and is equally at home (as all Range Rovers are) on or off the road. To make full use of its off-road properties, the Unitruck is often

Range Rover

used as an equivalent to a tractor for such tasks as crop spraying and broadcasting work, as well as general transport duties.

A plastic cover is available for covering up the rear, and the vehicle can be converted to take Liquid Petroleum Gas (LPG) instead of four-star petroleum.

To create extra space in the rear load area, the spare wheel is carried on a top roll bar on the roof. Also available are Land-Rover sand tyres for use on soft ground.

The Unitruck is certainly one of the most practical utility conversions based on the Range Rover.

London Taxis International,
Holyhead Road,
Coventry,
CV5 8JJ
(0203) 595001

CARE LE GANT

Care le Gant Upstage

The Upstage, constructed from fibre glass, is totally removable and does not damage

(so Care le Gant claim) or scratch the vehicle in any way.

The Upstage seats four people and there are spaces for a radio/cassette player, a radio telephone and storage lockers that can be constructed from teak woodwork.

To provide weather protection, either a waterproof tonneau or a sun canopy is fitted.

To get into the Upstage, a telescopic ladder is provided, which folds neatly into the base of the unit along with the covers and steel supporting rods for transportation.

The complete cost of the outfit is around £1580 including waterproof cover (at 1986 figures).

Care le Gant Limited,
59/61 Albert Embankment,
Vauxhall Cross,
London,
SE1 7TP
(01) 582 2202

The complete Upstage unit collapses into itself for travelling.

CARMICHAEL

Carmichael Commando R.I.V.

Based on the 6X4 chassis, developed by Carmichaels in 1970/1, the Commando R.I.V. (Rapid Intervention Vehicle) carries 200 gallons (90 litres) of premix foam solution, a crew of two, a 500 gpm at 100 psi pump (positioned at the front of the vehicle) and various assorted tools.

These tools are housed in capacious lockers, access to which is provided by steel roll-up side shutters.

The coachwork is constructed from aluminium alloy/glass reinforced plastic

The Commando features capacious ◆ lockers at the rear.

A Commando awaiting the addition of ◆ a custom-made rear body.

Range Rover

and is painted any colour requested.

Next to the front mounted pump, you will notice the extended front bumpers. These open to reveal small, but handy, lockers.

The Commando is used by many British and foreign airports, and can be redesigned to suit clients' requirements.

Length	5480 mm (216 in)
Wheelbase	3550 mm (140 in)
Height	2440 mm (96 in)

Carmichael Fire Limited,
Gregory's Mill Street,
Worcester,
WR3 8BE
(0905) 21381

Carmichael Clansman

Based, like the Commando, on the 6X4 chassis, the Clansman is really a six-wheel version of the standard Range Rover, with the exception of trim, colour choice and wheels.

The Clansman also used to be available in a 136-inch four-wheel version, but this was discontinued soon after launch.

The Clansman has quite an array of standard equipment fitted to it, these include external vinyl roof covering, power steering, all-terrain wheels and tyres and inertia rear seatbelts. With chrome bumpers, air conditioning, additional speakers in headrests, fully opening sunroof and chrome exhaust pipes

A typical six-wheel Carmichael Clansman. Note four-door conversion, three rows of seats and the roof extension.

14

positioned under the front doors as options.

An eighteen-gallon fuel tank, and roof extension are also often fitted, but are not standard.

Length	5370 mm (212 in)
Wheelbase	3440 mm (136 in)

Chameleon Six-Wheel. Note the sleek bull bar, roof extension and reshaped rear door.

CHAMELEON

Chameleon Long Wheelbases

Better known for their Mercedes conversions, Chameleon also convert Range Rovers, more often than not involving a stretch.

The 136-inch stretched four-door – which undoubtedly you will see again in this book – has all-terrain tyres and wheels, video, television, cocktail cabinet, refrigerator, interior retrim and folding 'occasional' seats.

Range Rover

Range Rover 136-inch four-door

The other stretched Range Rover by Chameleon is a truly enormous six-wheel version based on the four-door Range Rover. This particular version has an eight-inch roof extension, revised front end, sleek bull bar and all-terrain tyres.

Both vehicles were for export.

MALCOLM COLE

Malcolm Cole XD25 Diesel

Malcolm Cole Limited is a small marine and automobile engine specialist based in Poole, Dorset, who have been installing Peugeot diesel engines into Range Rovers for quite some time.

Since the launch of the works diesel, Malcolm Cole, naturally, have not sold as many units as usual. But this conversion should still be attractive to owners of older Range Rovers who would like a fuel bill similar to a Ford Sierra 1.6.

The following is a miles-per-gallon comparison between the Range Rover V8 and the Malcolm Cole diesel:

Range Rover V8

@ 30 mph: 25 mpg

@ 50 mph: 25.5 mpg

@ 70 mph: 19 mpg

Peugeot XD25

@ 30 mph: 45 mpg

@ 50 mph: 32 mpg

@ 70 mph: 25 mpg

(N.B. All figures quoted by Malcolm Cole Limited)

Malcolm Cole Limited,
48 Hatch Pond Road,
Poole,
Dorset,
BH17 7JZ

Conversions

The Peugeot XD25 Diesel fits snugly into the Range Rover's engine bay.

Malcolm Cole Six-Wheel

When transporting a 36-foot powerboat along the roads of the South Coast, there are few alternatives to an articulated lorry, but Miss Pearlcorder (the name of the boat) has a six-wheeled Range Rover to pull her along.

The complete rig is the property of Salisbury businessman and powerboat driver Ray McEnhill who is assisted in his racing by Noel Edmunds.

Miss Pearlcorder was the first of a design by Brian Hendicott.

The Range Rover features a 250 horsepower twin turbocharged V8 engine,

Range Rover

a special suspension system which can level and lift the rig (similar to the Citroen system), airbrakes, slight roof extension and a fully opening sunroof.

The vehicle is based on the 6X4 chassis.

Length	5370 mm (212 in)
Wheelbase	3440 mm (136 in)

DALE

Dale Electric Stem-Lite

A very widely used system to provide instant light, the Stem-Lite, at the touch of a button, rises to a height of 2.5 metres above the vehicle.

The complete unit features flashing beacon and four 500 watt Halogen floodlights to illuminate an area approximately 33 metres around the unit.

You are probably thinking that all this is very well but some cabin space must be sacrificed to accommodate a telescopic mast. Well, fortunately, the Stem-Lite uses a NASA developed system in which the mast 'folds'. It works something like this: the mast is constructed of stainless steel so shaped that, when the mast is raised, the steel bends up into its natural shape. And, when the mast is motored down, the steel bends/rolls into a spool. This is housed in the base of the unit, therefore creating no cabin intrusion.

Dale Electric Limited,
Faraday House,
Eastfield,
Scarborough,
YO11 3UT
(0723) 584661

A Dale Stem-Lite illuminating a rather nasty accident in Hull (Hull Daily Mail).

F.L.M.

F.L.M. (Panelcraft) Convertible

The F.L.M. (Panelcraft) convertible hood is, of course power-operated. But, ˙surprise, surprise, it has not got the usual ten-inch stretch most manufacturers add to provide extra rear legroom.

With the hood raised, the vehicle looks stylish and sporty. But, when the hood release/lower button is pressed, the vehicle comes into its own . . .

You can order virtually any option, as you will see in the next vehicle.

You can also order a four-door convertible with fold-flat windscreen.

F.L.M. (Panelcraft) Convertible with eight-inch overhang extension

One of the more unusual looking Range Rover is part of the series of 'one-off' vehicles built by F.L.M.

The vehicle has new front and rear ends in an American flavour. But, despite all the exterior amendments, the interior is the main feature.

Inside this interior, there are Recaro seats (trimmed in blue and white leather), a 'C.B.' radio, redesigned walnut facia with leather steering wheel and headrests all round.

Surely this surpasses a Rolls-Royce?

Or am I putting my head on the chopping block?

Length	4770 mm (188 in)

F.L.M. (Panelcraft) Hunting Seats

To provide good all-round visibility when hunting, F.L.M. have devised a system which electronically lifts and lowers the front passenger and rear seats twenty-three inches off the Range Rover floor.

There are many different versions of the Hunting Range Rover: one on the normal 100-inch wheelbase, one on the 110-inch wheelbase and the other with an eight-inch rear overhang extension.

You can order all manner of specialist hunting equipment, for example: gun racks, falcon perches, winches, additional lighting, supplementary fuel tanks, refrigerator, compasses, 'C.B.' radios, bonnet and tailgate fasteners and all-terrain wheels and tyres.

Note the sloping grille on some models. This indicates a power-operated winch.

Hunting Range Rovers can be based on the two- or four-door Range Rover.

The F.L.M. elevating hunting seats. They rise 23 inches off the Range Rover floor. Note the slanting grille. This indicates a power-operated winch.

F.L.M. (Panelcraft) 110-inch 'Ultimate'

At the end of F.L.M.'s brochure, there is a vehicle badged as 'The Ultimate in Four-Wheel Drive Transportation'. I am not entirely convinced of this claim (the Townley Desert Ranger takes some beating), but it is interesting no doubt.

The vehicle is stretched, this time by a

Range Rover

modest ten inches (the length most two-door convertibles are stretched to provide extra legroom), and vehicles built before 1981 had F.L.M.'s four-door conversion built on to them as well.

On this particular vehicle, new front seats and facia panel were fitted, exterior brightwork was finished in chrome, B.F. Goodrich all-terrain tyres and wheels were added, as well as flagpole-mounted on the bonnet. Exterior spotlights and a rear spoiler placed above the tailgate rounded off the comprehensive equipment.

The vehicle, of course, went to the Middle East.

As well as the Ultimate, F.L.M. has produced 110-inch Police cars based on the Range Rover for Bahrain.

This 118-inch wheelbase Range Rover has a 5.7 litre engine, and oversize front and rear doors.

| Length | 4920 mm (186 in) |
| Wheelbase | 2330 mm (110 in) |

F.L.M. (Panelcraft) 118-inch 5.7 litre

This vehicle has a 5.7 litre Chevrolet engine, three rows of seats, an outsize bull bar and a slightly overdone ventilation system!

F.L.M. and Wood & Pickett are the only Range Rover conversion specialists to produce a 118-inch chassis/body extension, and the 118-inch is F.L.M.'s most popular model.

To use the eighteen inches to the full, F.L.M. add nine inches to each door, providing phenomenally easy access to the three rows of seats.

Unfortunately, putting three rows of seats in a shorter wheelbase than a 136-inch means that you lose your load space. So, if you want to seat eight in your car, you had better opt for F.L.M.'s six-door conversion!

The Chevrolet 5.7 litre engine is an option, but well advisable for a vehicle of that size.

Length	4920 mm (194 in)
Wheelbase	2990 mm (118 in)
Engine	Eight cylinder in vee formation
Bore	101.6 mm (4.4 in)
Stroke	88.4 mm (3.4 in)
Cubic Capacity	5733 cc
Compression Ratio	8.5:1
Max Power (DIN net)	154 kW (205 bhp) at 4000 rpm
Max Torque	280 lbf ft

F.L.M. (Panelcraft) 118-inch Six-Wheel

Surely near the ultimate in stretched Range Rovers. Not only does it have 118-inch chassis extension, but six wheels and six-wheel drive, which was pioneered by Scottorn Trailers.

The vehicle has many options and features, such as: three rows of seats, full-length sunroof, Land-Rover sand tyres and refrigerator.

Conversions

Although F.L.M. did not say, I would assume it has a Chevrolet 5.7 litre engine, to help move all that weight around the desert.

The price was undisclosed, but I would imagine that about £80,000 was asked.

Length	5820 mm (230 in)
Wheelbase	3130 mm (154 in)

F.L.M. (Panelcraft) Six-Door

For the man with six or more wives!

You could order a six-door before 1981 (when the works four-door was introduced), although it was based on F.L.M.'s four-door conversion. After finishing this stage, the vehicle was then stretched and an additional two doors were fixed to each side, making a very smart (and expensive) conversion.

The six-door conversion is extremely practical if you have a large family (one Middle Eastern family had one built specially to ferry their children to school), as the vehicle can seat eight, as well as giving normal load space.

An F.L.M. six-door Range Rover. For the man with six or more wives!

Flared wheel arches were fitted for all-terrain wheels and tyres.

Length	5370 mm (212 in)
Wheelbase	3440 mm (136 in)

F.L.M. (Panelcraft) Racal Communications Unit

Based on the four-door Range Rover, the Racal communications unit seems to have everything in it, except the kitchen sink!

The roofline is raised by approximately two feet and houses an air ventilation/air conditioning system and other electronics wizardry.

The rear seats face backwards in order to provide a seat for the operator of the unit.

Height	2400 mm (95 in)

A communication unit for military. The electronics inside were provided by Racal.

Range Rover

F.L.M. (Panelcraft) Colonel Gaddafi's Troop Review Car

A quite attractive landaulet-style Range Rover has now been shipped over to Lybia, and is currently being used as a troop review car for Colonel Gaddafi.

It has a crescent-shaped rear window, front 'moonroof', grab rail, and the gap between the rear seats for the Colonel to stand on. There is a box-like seat at the rear for Gaddafi to sit on when he becomes tired of standing

F.L.M. (Panelcraft) Personnel Carrier

Built by F.L.M., this personnel carrier is based on the two-door Range Rover minus the roof, and can seat eight people (two in the front, six at the back).

To replace the sawn-off roof, a canvas

F.L.M.'S personnel carrier. This vehicle features fold-flat windscreen, sand tyres and fold-down rear step.

Interior of the Abu Dhabian Royal Guard Car. Note the leopardskin seats, machine gun post and wood strip all around the top of the body.

detachable hood with roll up/roll down side curtains is fitted, and if you wish you can order a fold-flat windscreen (fitted in this version). Many options are available for this conversion, such as machine gun and machine gun post, Land Rover sand tyres, rear step for easy access into vehicle, choice of upholstered seats and extra fuel and water tanks.

A coat of arms is on the door.

F.L.M. (Panelcraft) Abu Dhabian Royal Guard Car

Built by F.L.M. for the Abu Dhabian government as a guard car for the royal family.

The car is really a special version of the F.L.M. personnel carrier, with leopardskin seats, a machine gun post, extra fuel and water tanks, grab rails for security staff, Land Rover sand tyres and a fold-flat windscreen.

Other features include running boards and woodwork on the exterior of the vehicle.

F.L.M. Panelcraft Limited,
32 to 35 The Arches,
Broughton Street,
London,
SW8
(01) 622 2080

GLENFROME

The F.L.M. Abu Dhabian Royal Guard Car.

Glenfrome's Ashton. Seen here with hood raised.

Glenfrome Ashton

Following the F.L.M. convertible, at first glance the Ashton may look extremely similar, but, in many ways, it is extremely different.

Firstly, the Glenfrome has a ten-inch stretch (although early versions did not) and secondly, Glenfrome's version can be ordered with Glenfrome's unique front lights and grille.

The Ashton is a luxury four/five-seater which features a power-operated hood to provide luxury open air motoring any-where, on or off the road.

A range of interiors is offered, or you can specify your own. One client had mock zebra skin trim.

Range Rover

Glenfrome Ashton. There is still considerable luggage space, despite the convertible roof.

As well as specifying your own interior, you can also specify your own front end. One client had an eight-inch headlight mock Bentley grille style which was displayed at the 1983 Motorfair.

Length	4730 mm (186 in)
Wheelbase	280 mm (110 in)

Glenfrome Filton 109-inch

The Filton has a nine-inch chassis extension, putting it in line with the Glenfrome Ashton.

The advantages of the extra nine inches are an easier rear seat access and nine inches extra legroom for the rear seat passengers.

Of course, most of the Filtons Glenfrome has produced are to de-luxe specifications featuring interior retrims, front end treatments, all-terrain tyres and occasionally a radio telephone.

This is the smallest of a family of stretched Range Rovers.

Length	4700 mm (185 in)
Wheelbase	2770 mm (109 in)

Glenfrome Clifton 124-inch

The second-smallest of the range of stretched Range Rovers by Glenfrome, the Clifton, is stretched by 24 inches.

The 24 inches are put to good use by providing extra legroom and other amenities ranging from television and video to refrigerator and individual air conditioning.

The various features built on particular vehicles include double 'moonroof', walnut veneer/leather interior, all-terrain tyres, chromed front end and intricate coachline.

Length	5070 mm (200 in)
Wheelbase	3140 mm (124 in)

Glenfrome Dyrham

The Dyrham is virtually a notchback version of the Clifton, as it shares the same wheelbase and interior, but has a boot.

The vehicle has a specially reconstructed rear window, which is considerably smaller than the original, all-terrain tyres, and a boot which shares the same format as the Ashton.

As well as being based on the 124-inch chassis, the Dyrham can also be based on the 133 inch Westbury chassis.

Length	5310 mm (209 in)
Wheelbase	3380 mm (133 in)

Conversions

Glenfrome Westbury 133-inch

Similar in some respects to the Clifton, the Westbury differs by an additional 33 inches in length to afford even more legroom, 'occasional' seats, television, video, refrigerator and a radio/cassette player.

A choice of front ends, colours, interior furnishings (one client had a shower!), wheels and seating material is offered.

To use the 33 inches to the full, Glenfrome stretch the rear door, thus providing superb access in or out of the vehicle. The front door, however, remains the same size.

Length	5310 mm (209 in)
Wheelbase	3380 mm (133 in)

Glenfrome Portway 136-inch

A vehicle for the woman with six or more husbands!

Interior of the Portway, showing the three rows of seats.

This six-door, three feet longer Range Rover can seat up to twelve people (only with additional seating fitted in the rear load area of the vehicle).

If you are worried when you take delivery of your Portway that it will sag down and snap in the middle, then don't! Glenfrome claim that the Portway is probably stronger than the original car.

The occupants are treated to opulent luxury with many options, such as one headrest per person (six), restyled interior, full-length sunroof, air conditioning and a fridge/freezer for the rear compartment.

Length	5370 mm (212 in)
Wheelbase	3440 mm (136 in)

Glenfrome Six

Based on the 6x4 chassis (most six-wheel Range Rovers are) the Six can be rebodied to any desirable shape. i.e. pick-up, roof extension, hunting vehicle etc. You can also order six-wheel drive.

One owner of a rather battered

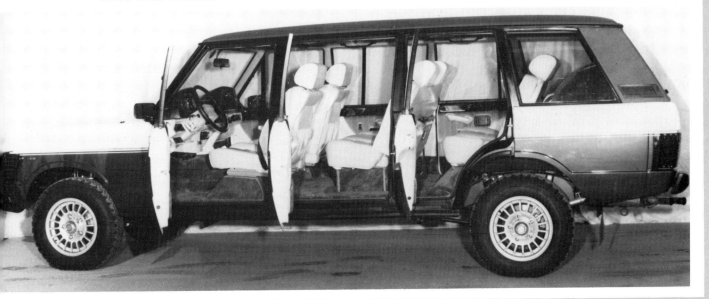

Range Rover

This Glenfrome Six has three rows of seats, and a slight roof extension.

Glenfrome Six pick-up with special wing mirrors, bull bar and flared wheel arches.

Glenfrome Six is BBC Radio One. This is used for towing a caravan with the Radio One Roadshow. Features on Radio One's vehicle include: Glenrover 'HL' front end, all-terrain wheels and tyres; interior retrim, full-length sunroof and rubber 'anti-knock' side strips.

Length	5370 mm (212 in)
Wheelbase	3440 mm (136 in)

Glenfrome Saha 6/Gulfstream

This rather unusual Range Rover was built as a hunting vehicle for the Malayan government.

Called the Saha 6, it featured a ten-inch stretch as well as the 36 inches created by the extra wheel, television, video, refrigerator, elevating hunting seats (similar to F.L.M.'s) amd a retrimmed interior in yellow and red.

The body is rather similar to a vehicle Glenfrome produced called the Gulfstream. This vehicle had a new front end, redesigned wheel arches and a redesigned roofline.

A few months after taking delivery of the Saha 6, the Malayans sent the vehicle back for a complete refit; it was later resold by Symbol of London.

Length	5620 mm (222 in)
Wheelbase	3690 mm (146 in)

The Saha 6

Conversions

Glenfrome Falcon Two-Door

The Falcon is a two-door, open-top hunting vehicle, which can also be used as a military patrol car.

The vehicle features fold-flat windscreen, roll-over hoop, jerry cans, long range petrol and water tanks, full canvas roof with side screens, side-facing rear seats and machine gun post (military patrol version only).

The military patrol vehicle pictured has all the above as well as half bench seats and a coat of arms in Arabic on the front door.

Also available is the special review version with rear seats twelve inches higher than standard.

Glenfrome Falcon Four-Door

Almost identical to the Falcon two-door, the Falcon four-door differs in the number of doors and the original rear seat instead of full length bench seats.

The vehicle has fold-flat windscreen, full canvas roof, removable roll-over hoop and half bench seats.

Extra fuel and water tanks are available as an option at extra cost.

Glenfrome Hawk

Similar to the two-door Falcon, with the exception of the truck-style cab to protect driver and passenger from the elements.

The Hawk's specification includes an open back with side-facing seats (no canvas roof supplied), strong roll-over cage, side hinged rear door, long range fuel tank, fresh water tank, fold down rear step (from Land-Rover Station Wagon), flared wheel arches and Kelly Safari RVR tyres.

A bull bar, aditional lighting and roof mounted spare wheel can also be fitted.

Glenfrome Hunting Specification

As the Arab oil magnates and royal families are rather partial to hunting with hawks and

The Glenfrome Falcon two-door.

The Hawk's rear compartment, showing the side facing seats and side opening rear door.

falcons, Glenfrome have developed many options built exclusively to aid desert hunting.

The first is a hawk-perch. This is trimmed in coarse grained leather and features dirt tray, adjustable tail support and leash clips. This can be removed when not in use.

The vehicle in which the hawk-perch was fitted was a standard four-door with the exception of elevating front passenger seat,

Range Rover

fold-back half-length sunroof, roof mounted front grab rail, two rear jerry cans and a custom-made half-length roof rack.

Falconry radar equipment can also be fitted. This device is dashboard mounted or portable and features a hand-held or vehicle mounted aerial and is capable of locating the direction of the falcon and indicating if the bird is in flight or on the ground.

To complete the range of Glenfrome hunting aids, there is the power winch, specially mounted to an extended bumper.

The vehicle also features chrome grille and light surrounds. The headlights have been waterproofed also.

Glenfrome Ceremonial Review

Renowned for their expertise in creating unique and individual vehicles, Glenfrome was commissioned to produce this review car for an undisclosed government (the car is a right-hand drive though).

Based on the four-door Range Rover (even though the car is a two-door), the vehicle creates a mobile dais for the reviewing of military exercises, parades and state occasions.

The vehicle has black leather seats, roof mounted flagpole, grab rails, red deep-pile carpet, fixed stairway and elevated platform for the reviewer to stand on.

Glenfrome Facet

The Glenfrome Facet, designed by Dennis Adams (Marcos Mantula designer), is described as the 'Ultimate All Terrain Sports Coupe'. It is based on the Range Rover chassis, with retrimmed interior which comprises leather seats and walnut veneer and an electrically operated rear window. The boot is electrically operated too. This can stow away the targa style roof (à la Fiat X1/9).

To start off with, the Facet had Vauxhall Cavalier headlights, but these were discontinued after a few months, and I think

Glenfrome's angular Facet. The body was designed by Denis Adams.

the current quadruple round headlights look better.

Some time in the future, there may be six-wheel Facets with full-length, gull-wing doors, but not until one of the Sheikh owners becomes bored with the present Facet's shape and orders one.

Glenfrome Interiors

To complement the superb exterior bodywork, Glenfrome has a range of interior features. These range from redesigned facias to additional seating.

A typical 'stretch' interior will feature television, video, fridge, additional seating, cocktail cabinet and air conditioning as well as the usual leather and walnut.

'Occasional' seats are small fold-away seats positioned just in front of the standard rear seat, and are only big enough to seat children, or small adults, as there really is not much legroom.

Alternatively, you can fit boot mounted 'occasional' seats. These, naturally, fit into the boot, and are big enough to seat, once again, children only.

Glenfrome Engineering Limited,
Imperial Works,
Hudds Vale Road,
St. George,
Bristol,
BS5 7HY
(0272) 55727

GLOSTER SARO

Gloster Saro 6X4 R.I.V.

Based on the 6X4 chassis configuration, the Gloster Saro is in many ways similar to the Carmichael Commando, with the exception of four doors, a higher roofline over the crew cab, and different rear coach work.

The tank, positioned over the two rear axles, has a maximum capacity of 200 gallons, and is made of glass reinforced plastic. It can either be connected to a monitor or a hosepipe. Tools are specified by the relevant authority.

Among the many airports, fire services and organisations around the world who buy them, the British Armed Forces is the biggest customer to date.

Length	5480 mm (216 in)
Wheelbase	3550 mm (140 in)
Height	2440 mm (96 in)

Note the front crash bar, and roof-mounted foam monitor on this Gloster Saro.

Gloster Saro Command Unit

Based on the Range Rover chassis, with a ten-inch stretch, and a body similar to an ambulance, the Fire Command Unit has many features including air conditioning, double spotlights, American style beacon, flashing front grille lights, Dale Stem-Lite, radio and other communications equipment needed for airport rescue command units.

Length	4927 mm (194 in)
Wheelbase	3000 mm (110 in)
Height	2133 mm (84 in)

Gloster Saro Limited,
Hucclecote,
Gloucester,
GL3 4AD
(0452) 69321

Gloster Saro Command Unit. Note the Dale Stem-Lite.

Range Rover

JANSPEED ENGINEERING

Janspeed Turbocharged Range Rover

One of the leading turbocharging specialists, Janspeed produce a super performance turbocharged conversion based on the standard Range Rover engine.

The new second generation blowthrough turbocharger system, whether single or twin turbo, utilises the standard Stromberg carburettor coupled to a baffled plenum chamber. Boost pressure is supplied on demand by either a single TO4 turbocharger or two Roto Master RM60 units producing 220 bhp.

As well as this conversion, Janspeed fit suspension, wheels and tyres as well as bull bars on Range Rovers.

Janspeed Engineering Limited,
Castle Road,
Salisbury,
Wiltshire,
SP1 3SQ
(0722) 21833

Janspeed Twin Turbo Range Rover.
The performance is stunning.

J.N.R. MOTORS GROUP

J.N.R. (Motors Group) Reveller

The J.N.R. Reveller range comprises four vehicles: the two-door, four-door, pick-up and six-wheel recovery vehicle.

The two- and four-door vehicles are really just Range Rovers with an additional axle, although this addition does have its advantages, for example extra traction and roadholding, the option of six-wheel drive, and extra loadspace.

Also available is an interior retrim.

The more utility side of the Range Rover Reveller, the pick-up offers enormous load space, with the comfort of the saloon model. Access to the pick-up area is via the rear tailgate, with a bed length of 96 inches (220 cm), with a total load area of 42 sq ft.

The recovery vehicle is very similar to the pick-up, with the exception of the crew cab and winch.

The winch is a Harvey Frost, which can front-lift and tow any family saloon car over varying types of terrain.

The only six-wheel drive ice cream van in the world! Built by J.N.R. Motors group, it can be found on the beaches of Wales.

Conversions

J.N.R. also build stretched four-wheel Range Rovers.

Length	5370 mm (212 in)
Wheelbase	3440 mm (136 in)

J.N.R. Motors Group,
Wainwright Street,
Aston,
Birmingham 6
(021) 328 0102

Chassis of the 6X6 ice cream van. Note the eighteen-inch extension.

As well as providing seating for four/five, this Reveller also gives ample luggage space, although outside.

One of the J.N.R recovery vehicles. The cab ensures seating for five people, and the winch is a Harvey Frost.

Range Rover

HERBET LOMAS

Herbet Lomas 110-inch Ambulance

The Lomas 110-inch chassis ambulance is based on the normal two-door, except, as its name suggests, it has a ten-inch stretch.

In addition to the stretch, even more interior room is provided by stretching the rear overhang by eight inches.

Inside the vehicle a variety of interior layouts is offered, ranging from seating to different stretcher arrangements, to a unique interior built to customer specification.

Featured in the vehicle is the unique Lomas 'Easy Loading Stretcher' which, in short, is a stretcher that can be loaded without the attendant having to enter the vehicle.

Length	4927 mm (194 in)
Wheelbase	2790 mm (110 in)
Height	2133 mm (84 in)

Herbet Lomas 135-inch Ambulance

The 135-inch ambulance is virtually the same as the 110-inch, with the exception of body and chassis length.

A side door is placed on the left- or

Interior of the Lomas 110-inch ambulance.

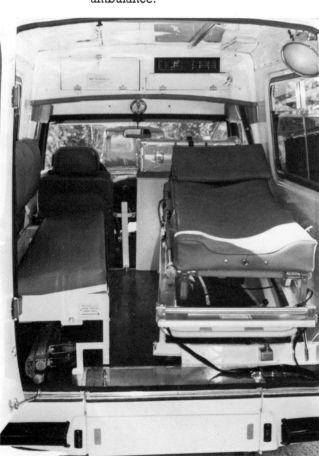

The Lomas 135-inch wheelbase ambulance.

Conversions

The Care le Gant Upstage. ◄

Hurn Airport's Carmichael Commando (Author). ►

Malcolm Cole six-wheel pulling Miss Pearlcorder. ▼

The Dale Stem-Lite rises to a height of 10 feet above the vehicle.

Interior of the F.L.M. (Panelcraft) convertible with eight-inch overhang extension.

The Scottorn Trailers 6X6. This provides superb off-road traction.

The Somerset Ambulance Control Unit. Based on the Lomas 110-inch Ambulance (Author).

The Queen's Royal Flight Gloster Saro R.I.V. There are two such vehicles. (Les. Dyke).

The ultimate hunting Range Rover. ⬆
A.E. Smith's 135-inch two-door hunting vehicle. The seats have bullet-proof backs.

The hunting vehicle with the roof raised. Note the extended bumpers. ⬇

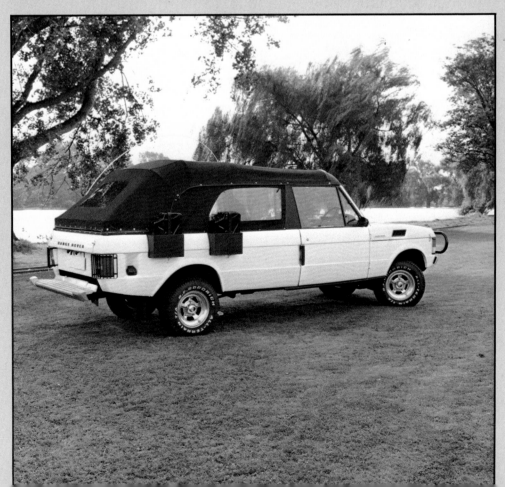

The Special Vehicle Conversions two-door Convertible.

Another Starlight. This time fitted with a square headlight conversion.

The ultimate converted Range Rover – the Townley Desert Ranger.

Ranger Rover fitted with velour-upholstered Recaro seats, and an incredible stereo system.

Six-wheel Desert Ranger interiors are royal throne room proportions ....

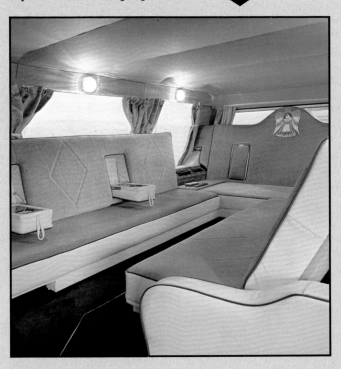

Boot mounted cocktail cabinet. It doesn't feature a 'Think before you drink before you drive' sticker however!

Wadham Stringer 110-inch wheelbase ambulance.

The attractive Sheer Rover 'S' front end. Basically, this is the lights from a Rover SD1 in thermoplastic rubber.

Wood & Pickett Sheer Rover, with various accessories. Featured are: custom 'paint job', bull bar, front spoiler, flared wheel arches, and all-terrain wheels and tyres.

The Newmarket Hunter is a more specialised hunting version of the Multi-Role.

The Sheer 'S' front end. Featured on this vehicle is a special front spoiler.

Comprehensive equipment fitted inside the Brinck Range Rover.

The body panels are added, and a reshaped front door is placed behind the original.

Range Rover

The American specification Range ⬆
Rover.
Ranger Rovers don't mind getting
their feet wet.
Range Rover with apt number plate
(ACTION). ⬇

right-hand side, and again you can specify your own interior, except that this time it can be larger.

Of course, having the extra 25 inches means that the asking price has almost doubled.

One Lomas 'Easy Loading' stretcher is fitted as standard, with a second emergency stretcher positioned beside it.

Length	5664 mm (223 in)
Wheelbase	3429 mm (135 in)
Height	2184 mm (86 in)

Herbert Lomas (Ambulances) Limited,
Unit Nine,
Radnor Part Industrial Estate,
Congleton,
Cheshire,
CW12 4XJ
(0260) 270013

OGLE DESIGN

Ogle Popemobile

The visit of His Holiness Pope John-Paul II to Britain in May 1982 required ceremonial transport that could fill special criteria.

To satisfy these requirements, Ogle converted four vehicles, two of them based on the Range Rover, the other two based on the six-wheel Leyland Constructor. They were both designed and built in less than four months.

The vehicles fulfilled their function so well that Pope John-Paul asked to take a Range Rover home with him.

Features include armoured glass in the rear (up to shoulder height), 'run flat' tyres, grab rails for security, special front bumper, step at the rear for use by security and bench seats in the rear.

Ogle Popemobile. The glass in the rear is bullet-proof up to 'shoulder height'.

Height	2700 mm (107 in)

Ogle Design Limited,
Birds Hill,
Letchworth,
Hertfordshire,
SG61 1JA
(0462) 682661

OVERFINCH

Overfinch 5.7 litre Engine Conversion

Distinguished by its special grille and side extractor panels, the Overfinch (formerly Schuler Presses) 57OT engine conversion offers the comfort of the standard Range Rover, but with more than ample power.

The vehicle is powered by the Chevrolet 5.7 litre engine, which is coupled to the GM 400 automatic gearbox (as used by Rolls-Royce and Ferrari).

Overfinch also convert the Range Rover's transmission and chassis.

The chassis modification offers improved off-road performance and cornering.

Range Rover

Overfinch add a revised grille to their 5.7 litre engine conversions.

In a test comparing cornering performance, the Overfinch Range Rover (0.85 g) came first overall over the Porsche 928 (0.83 g), Ferrari 308 GTB (0.82 g), Audi Quattro (0.72 g), Volkswagen Golf GTi (0.76 g) and the standard Range Rover (0.71 g).

Overfinch also offer a unique design and development facility for specialist vehicles, making their vehicles one of the most tested specialist vehicles on the road.
* N.B. All figures quoted by Overfinch Limited

Engine	
Eight cylinders in vee formation.	
Bore	101.6 mm (4.4 in)
Stroke	88.4 mm (3.4 in)
Cubic capacity	5733 cc
Max Power (DIN net)	154 kW (209 bhp at 4000 rpm)
Max torque	280 lbf ft

Overfinch Limited,
Unit 9,
Kingsland Industrial Park,
Bilton Road,
Basingstoke,
Hampshire,
RG24 0UB
(0256) 479490

PANTHER

Panther Convertible

Unfortunately, Panther are no longer producing converted Range Rovers, as all their resources are being allocated to new projects, like the Solo.

Panther has made some of the most luxurious conversions based on the Range Rover, for example the widened and stretched Range Rovers, six-wheel Range Rovers and this convertible.

Based, as usual, on the two-door Range Rover, this convertible does not have a ten-inch stretch. Naturally, the hood is power-operated, and this vehicle is fitted with all-terrain wheels and tyres.

Panther Convertible. Note the leather retrimmed seats.

Conversions

Although having 'ordinary' Range Rover seats, Panther have re-upholstered them with leather, and have fitted the rest of the interior with burr walnut to match.

Panther Widened Six Wheel

This fine example of the coachbuilder's art has been converted to be a foot wider, has elevating rear hunting seats, an extra set of wheels and a television, video, etc . . .

The extra twelve inches added to the width of the vehicle is achieved by adding six inches to each side of the bonnet and roof before reassembly. The axles are widened in a similar manner.

When you have all that weight to pull around, the normal Range Rover engine really does not provide sufficient power, so Panther can uprate the standard engine by 25%, although most conversions are fitted with 5.7 litre engines. But one client was still dissatisfied: he had a 6.5 litre installed.

Note the royal crest on the seats, and, although not shown in the photographs, this vehicle had three windscreen wipers!

Panther used to turn out ten Range Rovers a year, mostly going to the Middle East.

Mind you, at about £70,000 to £90,000 a throw, who else can afford it?

Length	5370 mm (212 in)
Wheelbase	3440 mm (136 in)
Width	2080 mm (82 in)

Panther six-wheel, with a slight chassis extension.

Range Rover

One of Panther's sumptuous interiors. It features video, television, leather seats, incredible stereo system and crystal decanter with matching glasses.

Panther Interior

This is the interior of a 136-inch wheelbase Range Rover with a slight roof extension. As you can see, it really has a de-luxe interior, featuring colour television, video, stero cassette deck with graphic equalisers, and headphones which all can be operated from a master remote control unit.

With all that electrical entertainment equipment, you need somewhere comfortable to watch and listen to it. To this end, Panther have fitted the interior completely with leather and walnut with reshaped seats (four of them in all) so you can relax in comfort. Further relaxation is supplied by the crystal decanter and glasses!

Is this the most mobile living room in the world?

The Panther Car Co.,
Brooklands Industrial Park,
Byfleet,
Weybridge,
Surrey,
KT13 0YU
(09323) 54066

PILCHER GREENE

Pilcher Greene SA/CS Ambulance

The four-wheel-drive power of the Range Rover, coupled to a sleek, capacious

Somerset's Pilcher Greene 110-inch Ambulance (Author).

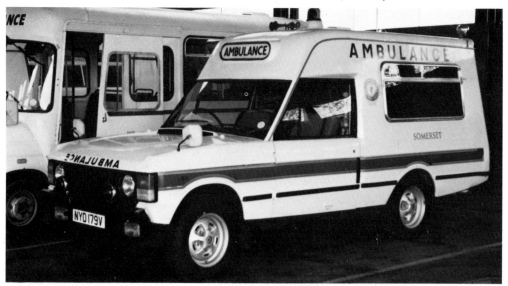

ambulance body complements the Pilcher Greene SA/CS Ambulance.

The vehicle is offered in two body styles, the SA and the CS. Although at first glance there does not seem to be much difference, the two ambulances are, in fact different in many ways.

Like the Lomas Ambulance, the vehicle is stretched by ten inches, and the rear overhang by eight, providing a very roomy interior. Access to this interior is via two rear doors, that open up 100 degrees, which are secured by a two-point vertical mechanism operated by the interior handle.

Pilcher Greene ambulances are very widely used in Britain, especially in remote hilly areas. There is one in service in Taunton, near the Quantock and Blackdown Hills, for example.

Length	4928 mm (194 in)
Wheelbase	2794 mm (110 in)
Height	2159 mm (85 in)

With four-wheel drive, the Pilcher Greene ambulance can go just about anywhere.

RAPPORT

Rapport Excelsior

Although Rapport is now part of the Symbol Group, and this model is no longer made, I feel this grotesque limousine should be included.

The Rapport Excelsior. The vehicle has a mock Rolls-Royce grille.

The Rapport 'Droop Snoot' bonnet.

This was Rapport's ultimate Range Rover. Stretched to provide eight-seat comfort (the occupants enjoy armchair-like seats), the vehicle can be fitted with elevating hunting seats, usual television, video, fridge, bar etc . . .

The vehicle pictured was fitted with dummy hood irons, outsize rear door and wide wheels.

As well as the above, a 'regal aspect' front end is fitted. This comprises a chrome bumper and light surrounds plus a mock Rolls-Royce style grille.

Dummy hood irons are fitted on the fixed head model or, if you prefer, the Excelsior can be made into a drop-top.

In fact, the Excelsior can be made into anything as long as the money lasts!

SCOTTORN TRAILERS

Scottorn Trailers 6X6

The Range Rover 6X6 all-wheel drive was developed by Scottorn Trailers in conjunction with Land-Rover in 1978 to meet an

The Scottorn Trailers six-wheel drive Range Rover.

ever increasing demand for a high powered cross-country vehicle with large passenger and cargo carrying capacity.

Drive to the rear axle is transmitted via the purpose-designed 'through drive' axle, which incorporates a vacuum operated lockable differential.

Ninety-nine per cent of all parts used in the 6X6 are either standard or modified Range Rover items, so producing a vehicle of Land-Rover standards.

As well as the four-door six-wheel Range Rover, special bodies can be fitted. These

All Scottorn 6X6 Range Rovers had four-door conversions, to provide easier access.

Range Rover

range from fire tenders to racing team vehicles, to rescue vehicles to military applications. The list is endless.

One such specialist body I must mention, is the 6X6 Reconnaissance Vehicle, for use in the desert. The vehicle is fitted with Land-Rover sand tyres, fold-flat windscreen, side jerry cans, machine guns and revised rear body.

The standard 6X6 is approved by the Ministry of Defence.

Length	5360 mm (211 in)	
Wheelbase	3479 mm (137 in)	

Reynolds Boughton Limited,
Scottorn Division,
Amersham,
Bucks,
HP6 6PE
(02404) 4411

A.E. SMITH

A.E. Smith Two-Door Convertible

Based on the two-door, the A.E. Smith convertible looks very stylish but, unlike

most of the Range Rover convertibles, the roof is not power-operated.

The two-door is first stretched by ten inches (A.E. Smith do this by adding ten inches to the chassis, then putting a completely reshaped rear wing in place of the standard item), next, the roof is cut off and moved up to the middle 'B' pillar.

The interior can be retrimmed.

Length	4720 mm (186 in)	
Wheelbase	2790 mm (110 in)	

A.E. Smith Four-Door Convertible

Unlike the two-door convertible entirely, the four-door has no hood, no ten-inch extension and a larger roll cage.

Based on the Vogue Range Rover, A.E. Smith firstly cut the roof off and totally redesign the 'C' pillar.

The four-door convertible has an attractive wedge-shaped look about it, but, unlike similar looking four-door convertibles produced by other companies, the A.E. Smith version has no roll bar. Instead,

The 110-inch convertible with the hood raised.

Conversions

A.E. Smith's attractive wedge-shaped four-door convertible. It has no canvas roof.

the standard 'A' and 'B' pillars are retained, providing more than ample protection during a roll.

A.E. Smith eight-inch Roof Extension

Why anyone would want to raise their Range Rover's roofline, I do not know. Anyhow, here is A.E. Smith's version.

With the roofline raised by approximately eight inches, the vehicle can accommodate some very tall people!

Based on the Vogue, the vehicle's interior is as standard.

A.E. Smith achieve the eight-inch extension by 'chopping' the standard roof off, and then attaching the new reconstructed roof on to the vehicle.

Height	2000 mm (79 in)

A.E. Smith Closed-Circuit Television Units

Built for security purposes, this Range Rover features a 36-inch roof extension, to accommodate a video camera on a telescopic mast. The mast elevates to thirty feet.

The vehicle was commissioned by the White Group, who specialise in mobile closed-circuit television units.

The vehicle features two television units, video recorder, complete control unit, two handy lockable lockers, side facing seat (based on the original rear seat) and a floor mounted spare wheel.

Also featured on this vehicle is a very apt number plate!

The second closed circuit-television unit differs only in its roofline. Instead of having an all-round 36-inch roof extension, this version has it only where the camera is housed.

A.E. Smith closed-circuit television unit, showing control panel and twin monitors.

Range Rover

The camera elevates to thirty feet.

Rear view of the closed-circuit T.V. unit. The vehicle was destined for the Middle East.

This particular version was destined for the Middle East.

Height	2700 mm (106 in)

A.E. Smith 100-inch Four-Door

Before 1981, the only way to buy a Range Rover four-door was to go to a specialist coachbuilder, and they would build one for you based on the two-door.

Most of A.E. Smith's 100-inch wheelbase four-doors went to Wood & Pickett, as A.E. Smith were commmissioned to build some of Wood & Pickett's 100-inch four-doors.

Note the flared wheel arches on the vehicle pictured.

A.E. Smith Elevating Seat

Based on the 136-inch wheelbase, this elevating seat rises twenty-two inches off the Range Rover floor.

As well as being able to rise and descend, the seat can also swivel round to face the driver or the rear seat passengers.

Of course having an elevating seat fitted means that a sunroof is necessary. This particular version has a half-length power-operated sunroof complete with wind deflector.

The front passenger seat is the only seat that elevates in this version, the rear seat and driver's seat are as usual.

Length	5370 mm (212 in)
Wheelbase	3440 mm (136 in)

A.E. Smith 136-inch Four Door

A.E. Smith were the pioneers of the much copied 136-inch wheelbase four-door

Conversions

One of the first A.E. Smith stretched four-doors.

Range Rover, and have produced quite a few.

To create the vehicle, the chassis is first stretched by 36 inches. Then a second reshaped front door is fixed behind the original, and the original rear wing is refitted behind that, making a very sleek looking Range Rover.

All manner of specialist equipment can be fitted in the extra 36 inches, the most popular being 'occasional' seats.

A 136-inch Range Rover was the first Range Rover conversion A.E. Smith did.

Length	5370 mm (212 in)
Wheelbase	3440 mm (136 in)

A.E. Smith 136-inch Hunting Vehicle

This vehicle is a sort of mixture between the A.E. Smith convertible and the 136-inch wheelbase, making a very stylish landaulet-type vehicle.

The vehicle has elevating hunting seats to armchair proportions (the seats both have bullet-proof backs), hawk-perches, jerry cans, power-operated custom built roof and two-way radio.

The vehicle was for a client in Kuwait.

Length	5370 mm (212 in)
Wheelbase	3440 mm (136 in)

A.E. Smith Range Rovers

A.E. Smith do a variety of interior retrims and body options for the 100-inch Range Rover.

The first is a square headlight conversion with large spoiler and fluted grille. This was built for Glenfrome.

The second is a 'seat transplant'. The standard Range Rover front seats were swopped for Recaro-style seats. The rest of the vehicle remains standard.

The third vehicle has a revised front end, unique wheels, new coat of paint outside and an interior retrim in red and white Dralon.

A.E. Smith Limited,
Dalkeith Place,
Kettering,
Northants.
NN16 0BQ
(0536) 85238

ALAN SMITH

Alan Smith Donnington/Ascot Viewplatform

The Donnington one-piece tailgate has been designed to eliminate the process of clambering on hands and knees when trying to reach shopping luggage etc., caused by the two-piece tailgate system (if you are a Range Rover owner you will know what I mean).

The unit is constructed of aluminium, and is hinged at the top. Two gas-filled struts hold the door in place when up.

Range Rover

Alan Smith's answer to the Upstage. The cheaper Ascot viewplatform.

A Donnington tailgate was fitted to the Royal Leicester Infirmary's Flying Squad emergency Range Rover.

Similar in some respects to the Upstage, the Ascot Viewplatform fits nicely into the gutter mounts to provide a dais to shoot (camera and gun), view or hunt.

The conversion also doubles as a heavy duty roof-rack.

The above conversions can be fitted with numerous options supplied by Alan Smith. These range from bull bars, headlight conversions and 'exterior enhancement'.

Alan Smith Limited,
Manchester Street,
Derby,
DE3 3GA
(0332) 40606

ALVIN SMITH

Alvin Smith Strange Rover

This vehicle has been designed and built specially for off-road trials, and is basically a Range Rover chassis with a roll cage or special body fitted.

To supply power during the competition, a Chevrolet 5.7 litre engine is employed, and the tyres are special all-terrain radials fitted to the standard Vogue or special off-road wheels.

The full-bodied version has the standard front lights and grille, but, apart from that, the body is all Alvin Smith, although he has fitted a Triumph TR7 body to the Range Rover chassis. This was a mistake, however, as the TR7 body was too heavy for trials work.

The Donnington one-piece tailgate by Alan Smith. Why Land Rover have never fitted such a tailgate is surprising.

SUC two-door Range Rover convertible.

Conversions

The Strange Rover minus body panels. Note the aluminium body frame.

The four-door SVC convertible allows seating for four/five, as well as the 'wind in the hair' fun of open motoring.

Bucket seats give extra comfort during the rigorous trials.

The engine, standard or Chevrolet 5.7 litre, is mid-mounted.

Alvin Smith Limited,
Smith's Garage,
Wallis Wood,
Ockley,
Dorking,
Surrey
RH5 5RD
(030679) 396

SVC

SVC Range Rover Grand Tourer Convertibles

Available in either two- or four-door configuration, the Specialist Vehicle Conversions 'Grand Tourer' convertible conversion can be built onto any age Range Rover.

Range Rover

For a basic price of £2500, SVC 'cut' the roof off, fit an excellently fitting manually-operated roof (that stows behind the rear seats under its own cover), enclose the rear end of the Range Rover to create a modest luggage area (most of it is taken up by the homeless spare wheel), strengthen the side pillars and fit a sturdy roll cage from 80 x 40 mm mild steel.

If you want a touch more luxury, an extra £2500 secures a luxurious Connolly leather interior, with walnut door cappings, and an extensively modified dashboard, again in walnut.

SVC Limited,
Hendall Gate Farm,
Herons Ghyll,
Uckfield,
TN22 4BU
(082581) 3158

SYMBOL

Symbol Starlight Convertible

Symbol, who are normally associated with luxury Mercedes and Rolls-Royces destined for the Middle East, can supply a most stylish convertible in either two- or four-door configuration.

You can order all manner of specialist equipment. From interior retrims, wheels,

tyres, new front ends, to the 'droop snoot' bonnet (à la Rapport).

As well as the Starlight, Symbol produce the Falcon, a two-door hunting model with side facing rear bench seats, bull bar, rear step and optional sand tyres.

Neither vehicle features a ten-inch stretch.

Symbol Quadraporte

One of many long wheelbase four-door models produced by many specialist manufacturers.

The Symbol model is no exception in the luxury end with two televisions (one front, one rear), video, cocktail cabinet, additional seating, and a new feature – a sink!

The vehicle can be based on the two- or four-door, although I think the four-door looks more stylish.

The Quadraporte can be fitted with a bull bar, Land-Rover side steps, silver grab rails, all-terrain wheels and various length wheelbases.

Like the Starlight, the Quadraporte can be fitted with the 'droop snoot' bonnet and various front ends.

Symbol International Limited,
66 to 70 Park Lane,
Mayfair,
London W1
(01) 491 8888

Typical Starlight interior: walnut, leather and deep-pile carpets.

Symbol Quadraporte interior. As usual, walnut and leather are very much in evidence.

Typical Symbol 135-inch interior. Note the occasional folding seats, cabinets for television and fridge, video and a new feature: a sink!

Sumptuous facia of the same Range Rover. If you look carefully at the middle section, you will notice a television mounted above the automatic gearlever.

TOWNLEY

Townley Desert Ranger

Now this, surely, must be the ultimate in converted Range Rovers.

The Desert Ranger is widened by six inches (this alone costs the same as an Austin Metro), is stretched by eighteen and is available in six- or four-wheel configuration.

To widen the vehicle, Townley stretch the axle the required width and completely rebuild the bonnet and tailgate, as well as fitting a custom-made windscreen.

Six-wheel Desert Ranger. This and a four-wheel were ordered as a set.

118-inch Desert Ranger. Note the three rows of seats.

Range Rover

Typical Desert Ranger interior. Note the coat of arms embossed on the seat backs.

Desert Ranger interior. The roof is fully-opening to reveal television, video, and seating for eight.

Not satisfied with this, the client normally orders anything from a ten- to a twenty-inch stretch (depending on the size of his/her legs presumably) and a higher roofline.

As well as altering the exterior appearance, Townley also change the interior to royal throne room proportions to seat eight. To keep these eight people amused, a video, television, cocktail cabinet, telephone and complete hi-fi system are fitted.

Normally two Desert Rangers are ordered to make a set. These are normally a four-wheeler and a six-wheeler, so the client has the best of both worlds!

Length	5830 mm (230 in)
Wheelbase	3900 mm (154 in)
Width	3280 mm (76 in)
Height	2100 mm (83 in)

Townley Six-Wheel

A very adaptable firm, Townley produce a variety of six-wheelers based on the 6x4 or 6x6 chassis for hunting or domestic purposes.

These two Shaheens were ordered as a set.

The Hunter is the hunting version of the six-wheel. It features elevating seats, full-length sunroof, interior retrim, all-terrain tyres and front mounted winch.

The Shaheen was a 'one-off' six-wheeler, presumably built for a person of that name. The vehicle is a landaulet and has a revised front end, all-terrain tyres, elevating seats and an interior retrim. Note the rear door which has been shortened to provide extra body strength.

As well as the above special-bodied six-wheel Range Rovers, Townley can also supply six-wheel Range Rovers with standard bodies.

| Length | 5370 mm (212 in) |
| Wheelbase | 3440 mm (136 in) |

Townley Ranger

The Ranger is really an upmarket version of the Glenfrome Hawk, which features flared wheel arches, running boards, grab rails, middle partition, side facing seats, side-opening tailgate and all-terrain wheels and tyres.

Townley Six-Door

The Townley version of the six-door Range Rover is very similar to the Glenfrome and F.L.M. vehicles, but has only recently been made.

Townley manufacture the six-door by first stretching the chassis 36 inches, chopping the bodywork in half, and then adding a reshaped front door behind the original.

Interior retrims are usually included in the specification.

These are one of Townley's specialities, with a team of expert craftsmen in wood veneers and leather, working together to

Townley six-door Range Rover. Note the Windsor front end.

make some of the World's most luxurious interiors.

The facia is reconstructed, and the seats, steering wheel and doors are retrimmed in any colour leather to the clients' choice.

As well as retrimming the standard interior, Townley also make custom interiors to suit the clients' specifications.

Townley Convertible

Townley manufacture a wide variety of convertibles on both the two- and four-door Range Rovers.

The two-door model has all-terrain tyres, special front end, power-operated hood, interior retrim and running boards.

The four-door convertible is based on the Vogue and features power-operated hood, roll cage, rear headrests and fold-flat windscreen.

Some special models have been produced. For example: the Royal Saken. This features a special crescent-shaped rear window (similar to Colonel Gaddafi's review car), interior retrim, running boards, flared wheel arches (to accommodate all-terrain tyres), special front end and

Range Rover

Townley Royal Sakens. Note the reversed front door handles.

elevating front and rear seats for passengers only. The vehicle also features special door handles.

Townley Range Rovers

For the person who cannot afford such vehicles as the Desert Ranger, but who wants something a little more special than the 'standard' Range Rover, Townley have a range of options and accessories especially for the Range Rover.

These include a new coat of paint in any colour requested, all-terrain tyres, bull bars, full-length sunroof, chromed bumpers and light surrounds, flared wheel arches, running boards, new front ends and, of course, the Windsor interior retrim.

If you can't afford the Desert Ranger, how about a 'standard' Range Rover with an interior retrim, special paint job and a revised front end?

Conversions

WADHAM STRINGER

Wadham Stringer 110-inch Ambulance

Another ambulance, again on the 110-inch chassis, except this time with a totally different layout for the rear.

The two-stretcher layout features two Wadham Stringer Reasac stretcher trolleys, an attendant's seat, full-height partition with half sliding window and locker over the cab.

Wadham Stringer 110-inch wheelbase ambulance. Note the Dale Stem-Lite fitted.

The single-stretcher layout has no partition, and either two high back seats with armrests or a bench seat for three people can be fitted.

Unlike the Lomas and Pilcher Greene ambulances, the Wadham Stringer has a separate body and a twelve-inch rear overhang, not an eight-inch, making a truly monstrous vehicle, but still not the biggest ambulance.

Length	5030 mm (198 in)
Wheelbase	2784 mm (110 in)
Height	2184 mm (86 in)
Width	1803 mm (71 in)

Wadham Stringer 135-inch Ambulance

The largest ambulance based on the Range Rover, the Wadham Stringer 135-inch ambulance is similar to the 110-inch, with the exception of the additional 25 inches,

Range Rover

Wadham Stringer 135-inch. This vehicle is for export only.

and a fully opening side door positioned just after the front door.

As the vehicle is longer, more equipment can be fitted to the interior. This equipment is as follows: Two Wadham Stringer Reasac or two F.W. York II stretcher trolleys, a backrest with four folding armrests is fitted for sitting-case patients, two rear facing attendants tip-up seats on middle partition, two canvas stretchers and fluorescent lighting complete the standard equipment.

Options include: carrying chair, air conditioning and resuscitation and oxygen units.

Length	5640 mm (223 in)
Wheelbase	3394 mm (135 in)
Height	2184 mm (86 in)
Width	1803 mm (71 in)

Wadham Stringer (Ambulances) Limited,
Hambledon Road,
Waterlooville,
PO7 7UA
(07041) 58211

WOOD & PICKETT

Wood & Pickett Aintree Multi-Role

As the name suggests, the Aintree Multi-Role Sheer Rover is truly a 'Multi-Role' vehicle.

Designed by Ogle, the vehicle has numerous features, such as fold-flat windscreen, removable targa roof panel, removable vinyl cover for the rear, storage boxes under the rear bench seats, front bumper capping (similar to the Ogle designed Popemobile), flared wheel arches, running boards and side grab handles.

The vehicle makes an ideal desert hunter, desert 'dune hopper', ceremonial review or riot control vehicle.

Wood & Pickett Antree Multi-Role. The vehicle can be used for hunting, reviewing, riot control and personnel carrier.

The Multi-Role, designed by Ogle, shares the same front bumper as the Popemobile.

Range Rover

Wood & Pickett Goodwood Convertible

Based on the two- or four-door Range Rover, the Goodwood includes full power-operated hood in Mohair, a ten-inch stretch (behind the door on two-door models, and on the rear overhang on the four-door), flared wheel arches, running boards and interior retrim.

Both vehicles look extremely stylish, especially the four-door, with its strengthened roll cage and fluted grille.

Length	4730 mm (185 in)
Wheelbase	2800 mm (110 in)

Goodwood four-door. The ten-inch extension is placed in the rear overhang, to provide more luggage space.

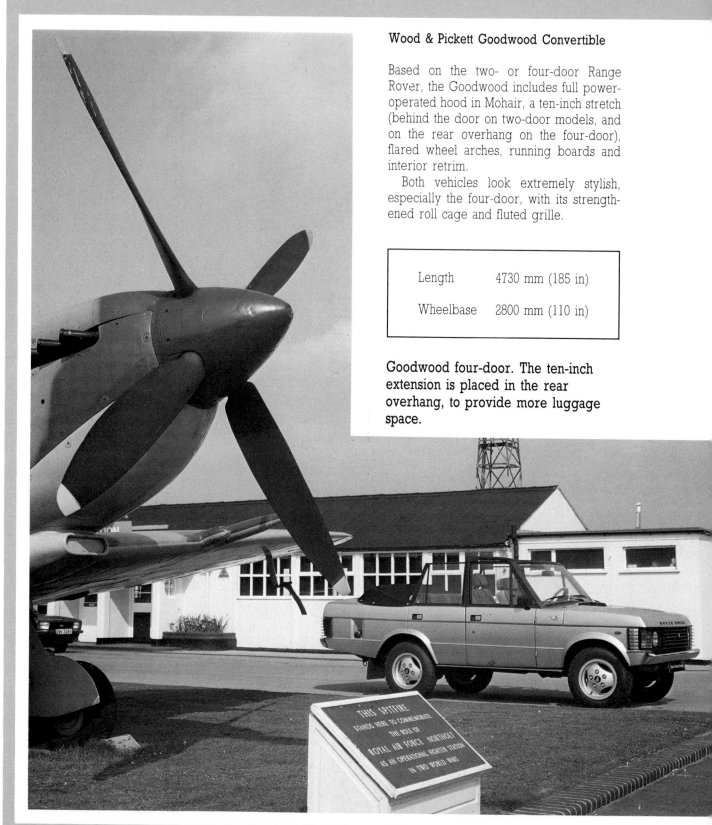

Conversions

Wood & Pickett Newbury Falcon

For the avid hunting enthusiast, the Newbury Falcon offers ultimate flexibility. The design incorporates the following: easily removable vinyl roof, padded outer frame, two fixed hunting seats (they do not elevate) that can be removed when not needed, seatbelts and falcon-perches.

If required an additional 34 litre petrol tank can be fitted and a Chevrolet 5.7 litre engine also.

The canvas roof is totally removable, and the rear seats six. ⬆ ⬇ Note the fixed elevated seats in this Newbury Falcon hunting vehicle.

Range Rover

Wood & Pickett Newmarket Hunter

A more luxurious, specialist hunting version of the Multi-Role, the Newmarket Hunter features a liftout glass 'moonroof', two full-length bench seats, side opening rear tailgate, vinyl roof covering with removable hood sticks and roll up/roll down side curtains, flared wheel arches, front spotlights and a long range petrol tank.

Note the fuel access cap has been removed from the side to the rear.

Options available to order.

Wood & Pickett Warwick

For people with slightly more than average length legs, Wood & Pickett produce the Warwick. Stretched by nine inches, this Range Rover provides just enough room for a television, video and cocktail cabinet.

Of course the Warwick is available with the various Wood & Pickett front ends, interior retrim, flared wheel arches and all-terrain wheels and tyres.

Length	4700 mm (185 in)
Wheelbase	2770 mm (109 in)

Wood & Pickett Epsom

For people with very long legs, Wood & Pickett produce the Epsom. Nine inches longer than the Warwick, this provides even more room for the extras, also a third row of seats can be squashed in.

Again, the usual Wood & Pickett options can be installed.

Length	4920 mm (194 in)
Wheelbase	2990 mm (118 in)

Wood & Pickett Ascot

Based on the four-door manual or automatic Range Rover, this particular Ascot has an 18-inch extension, a four-inch raised roofline, all-terrain tyres, interior retrim, television, video, bull bar and long range fuel and water tanks.

The four-inch roof extension can be incorporated in an ordinary four-door Range Rover without the 18-inch stretch.

Length	4920 mm (194 in)
Wheelbase	2990 mm (118 in)
Height	1900 mm (75 in)

Wood & Pickett Cheltenham 6

Based on the two- or four-door Range Rover, the Cheltenham 6 uses the 6x4 chassis configuration, and is available with all the usual options.

Before 1981, the Cheltenham was available in a four-door version which was firstly built by A.E. Smith. This was then sent back to Wood & Pickett for the addition of the third trailing rear axle.

Among the owners are Wolf Race wheels and tyres, who had one built for publicity purposes.

Length	5370 mm (212 in)
Wheelbase	3440 mm (136 in)

Wood & Pickett Windsor

For people who have a tendency to constantly wear stilts, Wood & Pickett

Conversions

Similar to the Rapport Excelsior, this Windsor had dummy hood irons and a mock Rolls-Royce grille. The 36-inch extension was carried out by A.E. Smith.

produce the Windsor. The grandest and longest long wheelbase produced by Wood & Pickett, the Windsor can be based on the two- or four-door Range Rover, and a variety of options can be fitted.

The Windsor pictured has a mock Rolls-Royce grille and dummy hood irons, making it similar to the Rapport Excelsior.

Length	5370 mm (212 in)
Wheelbase	3440 mm (136 in)

Wood & Pickett Front End Styling Options

Many front ends are offered by Wood & Pickett, including the 'S' front end, which is really the lights from the Rover SD1 incorporated in thermoplastic rubber.

The 'HL' front end is four Halogen quartz headlamps recessed in a horizontal grille, which is painted to the client's choice.

The 'H' grille was first introduced in 1976, and is the only grille of its type in the world (the companies that fit this grille purchase straight from Wood & Pickett).

The polka-dot grille of the Sheer Rover 'O' front end.

Range Rover

The 'O' grille is the last grille from the Wood & Pickett range. It is two square headlights alongside a polka-dot ventilation grille.

Of course, Wood & Pickett would be only too happy to create a grille to your specific design.

Wood & Pickett Interiors

To match the exterior amendments, Wood & Pickett have a range of interiors to suit your every need.

As Wood & Pickett are the UK importer of Recaro seats, these are normally featured in typical Wood & Pickett interiors.

To match the seats, Wood & Pickett normally fit the Margrave facia. This is a reshaped standard facia trimmed in leather, with revised instruments and a new steering wheel.

The interior can be trimmed in leather or Dralon, and the colour is up to the customer.

Also featured in many an interior is the centre mounted television positioned in a centre console. The vehicle does not have to feature a stretch to accommodate this.

Wood & Pickett Longchamp

In direct competition with the Glenfrome Facet, the Wood & Pickett Longchamp is a completely redesigned body on a Range Rover chassis.

The vehicle has Recaro Orthopaedic Electric seats, interior retrim in leather or Dralon, Margrave facia panel in birds eye maple, video and television in rear centre console and fridge cooler in the rear of the vehicle.

This vehicle is a limited edition only, and each vehicle is issued with a personal number.

Wood & Pickett Limited,
40 Old London Road,
St. Albans,
Herts,
AL1 IT2
(0727) 41361

The ultimate Sheer Rover; the completely rebodied Longchamp (Peter Brooker).

Conversions

SPECIALIST USES

The Queen's Review Range Rover

Normally, the Queen uses a specialist Mulliner Park Ward Rolls-Royce Phantom for ceremonial drives, but occasionally she has to travel on softer ground. Here the heavy Rolls-Royce might sink, so a special Range Rover is used instead.

The vehicle is based on the two-door Range Rover, and is standard apart from the rear.

In this rear, special bench seats (well, more like armchairs) have been fitted, along with a specially padded roof frame and side opening rear door.

Several Range Rovers have been converted for the Queen and other members of the royal family. These follow in a long tradition of Land and Range Rovers used by the royals on both state and leisure occasions.

The Queen's Range Rover.

The Queen's review Range Rover. Naturally it does not have a number plate.

Range Rover

Automobile Association Range Rover

Unfortunately, the A.A. no longer operate Range Rovers, which were mainly based in the Highlands of Scotland.

The vehicles used by the Association were in no way mechanically different from those sold to the public, they were simply printed yellow at the factory, with A.A. livery, roof rack, beacons, illuminated A.A. sign, usual A.A. tool kit, radio and spotlights fitted at the A.A. headquarters.

The vehicle helped in many ways in the Highlands digging out snow-buried vehicles, helping the Police during accidents and, of course, repairing vehicles.

Thanks are due to the A.A. for supplying the photographs.

The A.A. digging out snow-stuck cars in the Highlands. The A.A. Range Rover doesn't get stuck.

Conversions

BBC Reception Survey Unit

To ensure that the reception in certain areas of the country is clear, the BBC employ two Range Rovers with special equipment inside.

The telescopic mast can elevate to a maximum height of thirty feet, and the vehicle also features radiophonic equipment, television and a heavy duty sunroof.

Also featured is a sink.

BBC reception survey unit. ◆ ◆ Inside the reception survey unit.

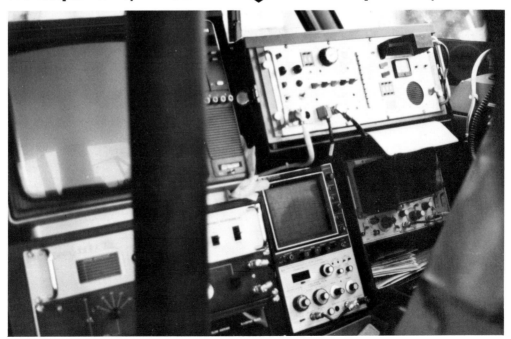

Range Rover

Range Rover Police

With the powerful V8 engine, four-wheel drive and excellent load-carrying capacity, the Range Rover is the ideal vehicle for the Police Force.

Based on the Fleetline Range Rover (the cheaper and more basic version), the Range Rover is in service with virtually every Police Force in Britain.

All Police Range Rovers are slightly different, depending on the Force's requirements. However, all Police Range Rovers have the same basic equipment. This includes side reflective strip, calibrated speedometers, map reading light, heavy duty batteries, roof mounted beacon(s) and spotlights (a Dale Stem-Lite can be fitted instead), a 10 channel VHF radio, 20 road cones, 12 blue flashing lights which

A Warwickshire Constabulary Range Rover fitted with a Dale Stem-Lite.

Conversions

Police Range Rover, with its stable mate, the Land-Rover 110.

fit into the cones, 'Police Accident', 'Police Slow' and directional signs, a 'Wide Load' sign that can be fitted on the bonnet, a two-tone horn or siren, fire extinguisher, shovel, brush, axe, crowbar, a tape measure, comprehensive first aid kit and a jerry can of water. Most of this equipment is fitted by the relevant force.

Some special versions have been produced, one being a four-door Range Rover used to transport criminals to the courts. This version incorporates blacked-out 'one-way' windows.

Occasionally a Police Force orders a Range Rover with the Janspeed Turbo conversion, which gives more power than the standard V8.

Police Forces choose the Range Rover for many reasons. For a start, the Range Rover has an excellent vantage position, thus giving unrivalled vision over cars in front, also, for the Range Rover's four-wheel drive capabilities. Police Range Rovers have been known to drive straight over accidents, when it has been impossible to drive around them.

On the Hammersmith Bridge, in rush hour, when a car breaks down, a City of London Police Range Rover with special rubber mounts on the bumpers pushes the luckless car and driver to the side, so normal traffic flow can be resumed.

On the M62 (the highest motorway in the British Isles), there is often extremely bad

Range Rover

weather. This means that accidents are unfortunately inevitable.

When this occurs the Policeman's job, apart from rescuing injured people, is to get the traffic flowing again as quickly as possible. To do this often involves towing cars, 32 ton articulated lorries (sometimes overturned) off the carriageway,

sometimes at night in the middle of a snowstorm.

The Range Rover is made for the job, and often does it, quickly and efficiently, proving that the Range Rover is probably the most ideal Police vehicle in service today.

Avon & Somerset Constabulary Range Rover (Author).

Much equipment is stored in the Range Rover's capacious boot (Author)